I0841216

THE UNNOTICED ADVANTAGE

ROY REDD

iii

ABOUT ROY REDD

Roy is a best selling author of the book The Success Magnet: Cultivate the 5 values that attract success. Roy also Is a performance coach who works with pro, college, and high school athletes. He works with the athletes to dramatically increase, tangible, measurable, and physical results. He also does this with companies, organizations and anyone who has a purpose.

At the age of 25, Roy realized he was not the person he wanted to become. That's when he decided to make a change in his life. Since that startling realization, he went from broke to making six-figures, homeless to buying his first home, and depressed to feeling fulfilled.

Roy Found that his distinctions dramatically increased what he calls workability. Workability simply means the ability to get the job done. When we look at the workability of an object we judge the object on its ability to do what the object was made for. With this knowledge, Roy realized that the workability of a human comes down to the human's ability to achieve its purpose. This makes performance the most important thing in life because to perform means to do what it takes to achieve a purpose. Roy became a performance coach for Pro, collegiate, and high school athletes. With a new distinction, Roy calls UnBounded Performance Roy is coaching people to dramatically increases tangible, measurable and physical results.

Roy has spoken at Ted, National Head Start Conference, International Health and Wealth conference, La Sierra University, Unbounded Basketball Camp, Chaffey College, Inland Empire One Love Christmas Party For Orphans, and Multiple High School, College, and NBA Teams. I have been featured on shows like Hollywood Unlocked, The daily Grind, Convos with Cole, and multiple radio shows and podcast.

Check out Roy's Ted Talk here: https://youtu.be/_9kQFw-Mcnw

www.RoyRedd.com

with Wayne Allyn Root
2008 presidential nominee

with Greg Reid author of
"6 Feet From Gold"

with Joseph Michelli author of
"The Starbucks Experience"

with Donna Karen

with Arnold Schwarzenegger

Table of Contents

THE UNNOTICED ADVANTAGE

THE SECRET REQUIREMENT THAT ORGANIZATIONS, TEAMS, AND ATHLETES NEED TO PERFORM AT THEIR PEAK POTENTIAL BEFORE SPORTS PSYCHOLOGY, LEADERSHIP SKILLS, STRENGTH TRAINING, TEAM BUILDING, AND TEAMWORK WILL EVEN WORK!!!

Why is it that some organizations thrive and perform while others simply do not? Why is it that some organizations succeed on a high level while others do not? Is it because those organizations are just better than the others? Have you ever looked at an organization that has more talent than another organization but is not performing nearly as well? Are you the owner or leader of a team or organization with a clear vision of how you can perform but, for some reason, aren't performing at that level? If you are, this short book is perfect for you. Most coaches, owners, and leaders have tons of ideas on how to improve performance, but none of them actually give access to performance itself. The problem is, the teams that actually do perform on a high level do not have any clue about how they are able to do this, so they come up with abstract ideas on how they were able to do it, such as: "We work hard," "We have integrity," or "We were lucky to be in the right place at the right time."

Luck is simply success that we do not know how to explain yet. In this book, we are going to give any leader the one and only secret to accessing the performance they desire for their team. This secret is very simple, but we have found that it is something the world can not see; it is a law of nature lingering in the background that is not in our awareness. This book will bring it into your awareness and also give you a tangible way to apply it to your system. I wish, for your benefit, I could charge you $10,000 for the info I'm giving in this book; that's how powerful it is, but if I charged that much, I doubt many people would read it. This book is worth $10,000 to you because it does not teach you anything new but actually gives you understanding and power from the knowledge you already have.

We all know people who have a head full of knowledge but no performance and results to go with it. So, instead of reading this book for more knowledge, please read it with the desire to understand what you already know. This is not a change in anything you are doing; it is simply something you must add to what you are already doing so that what you are doing can work. Without this secret, what you are doing to improve will not work, and that is a fact.

IF IT WORKS, IT WORKS; IF IT DOESN'T, IT DOESN'T

Science has a full set of rules and measurements that make flying and flight possible. Using physics and scientific laws, we were able to make vehicles that fly across the air. So, if we do not follow these laws of physics, will flight be impossible? Of course not. So, why is it that we try to stick to certain social paradigms on how things should be done? The bumblebee proves this point in a great way. Science, for years, had no clue how bumblebees are capable of flight. The way a bee is built and the way they flap their wings go against all the laws of physics. The first thing science notices about bees is that they do not look flight worthy. They have short stubby bodies and short wings which, with an eye test, makes the bee look incapable of flight.

As a coach or leader, have you ever looked at a team member, player, or peer with those same eyes? Have you ever thought that someone could not get a task done because they did not fit what you considered to be right? This is the biggest mistake that coaches make when they judge a player, or an owner when they hire staff members, or leaders when they organize a team. You, they, we have these ideas that keep us from giving ourselves and others the most important thing needed to see our potential—an opportunity. That is what this book is about.

This book gives people the opportunity set for performance. We will talk about what performance actually is, what performers do, and how to always have an opportunity for performance. We all have ideas on what performance is, and I am willing to bet that you are absolutely right about your idea on performance. But, and there is a big but, not all people are giving themselves the opportunity to allow the performance they desire to be present. As a coach, leader, team member is this: no idea matters; all that matters is the result that you are looking for, which leads me to my next point.

I walk around anywhere from four percent body fat to eight percent body fat, depending on what I choose to do in that time of my life. My dad, Eric Redd, trains NBA players, college athletes, high school phenoms, and also just your regular everyday person who wants to stay fit. My dad has trained guys like Allen Crabbe, who earned a seventy-five-million-dollar contract; Paul Pierce; Darius Morris, who played for the Lakers; and many, many more. My dad is one of the most knowledgeable trainers on the planet hands down. He can watch someone walk and tell you where they lack mobility, where they are tight, and what they need to do to create an adaptation for the result they want.

I notice that when I eat high-carb starchy foods such as donuts, I feel good, I look great, and it gives me tons of energy. Donuts are not healthy for you, and I am not saying that they are healthy for me, but I wonder why they have so many good effects on me. I asked my dad why this was, and he gave me two answers. The first answer was all the science and possibilities of what could be going on scientifically. He then started to tell me about guys who went on diets eating all McDonald's, and they lost weight. I gave him some pushback and said, "Well, that's not healthy," and he stopped me in my tracks. That's when my dad gave me the most powerful wisdom I have ever heard in my life, "Look, we study and learn what we can about the body, but we truly do not know how it works. I am not saying that it's healthy or it's not healthy, but I am saying it works. If it works, it works; and if it doesn't, it doesn't." This is truly the only fact in life, and I want you to be clear now that this is a concept you need to adopt moving forward if you want to increase your opportunity and potential for your performance as an athlete, team, or organization. "If it works, it works; and if it doesn't, it doesn't," and you can not know this until you increase your opportunity for performance.

WORKABILITY AND PERFORMANCE

Does it work? Did it work? Will it work? This needs to be your new judgment tool if performance, increasing potential, and achievement is what you are looking for. Coach's error comes from assessing with their ideas rather than their results. We are going to make distinctions that prove this point and show you how to access this concept so that you are not just left with ideas and you can actually know how to profit from this concept.

Now that we are assessing based on results instead of ideas, how do we make something work? How do we know that something is working? Well, let's look at an object like a hammer. How do we know if a hammer is working? We must know the hammer's purpose, right? Right. The purpose of a hammer is to drive nails into other objects. So, a hammer is working when it can do that task. The hammer is working when it can achieve its purpose, and a hammer can perform when it can do what it takes to do what it was made for. This idea is what we call 'workability.'

When something has workability, it simply means it works; and if it works, it can perform; and when it can perform, it will achieve its result like clockwork. This brings us to the law of performance. The law of performance says that as workability declines, performance declines; and when performance declines, the achievement of the result becomes more difficult, longer to achieve, or impossible to achieve based on the lack of workability.

> "As workability declines, performance declines;
> and when performance declines, the achievement
> of the result becomes more difficult, longer to
> achieve, or impossible to achieve based on the lack of
> workability."

Can you see why workability is so important now? Can you see why an opportunity for performance is so important? We talked about the workability of a hammer, but what is the workability of a person, a team, or an organization? If you can not answer that question, that is bad and also good. Bad because you literally have no way to manage if you have an opportunity for performance; good because when you make this distinction, you will become clear on how to literally increase your potential immediately.

INTEGRITY AND WORKABILITY

Take, for instance, the workability of a bicycle wheel, how do we know the wheel is working? By the wheel's ability to roll, right? Right. So, what will keep the wheel from performing? The wheel will lose its ability to work if it has physical damage such as if the tire loses air, the spokes in the middle are broken or lost, or if the inner tube has a hole in it. The wheel can not work when the wheel loses its integrity. Integrity is defined as being whole, complete and undivided. So, as the wheel loses its parts or becomes damaged, it loses its ability to work—because it loses integrity. So, now that we know this fact, let's add to our performance model.

The more undivided the wheel becomes, the less integrity the wheel will have; and as the wheel loses integrity, workability declines; and as workability declines, performance declines until it's so bad the wheel can no longer achieve its outcome. We know what material a bicycle wheel is made of; we also know the structure this material must be in so that the wheel can do its job; and lastly, we know what the purpose of a bicycle wheel is. We can apply this knowledge to individuals and organizations. We must know what people and organizations are made of, the purpose as well as the structure that allows workability for a person or team. We must know who we are, what our chosen purpose is, and where the structure of individuals exists.

THE PURPOSE OF A PERSON OR AN ORGANIZATION

Purpose is a huge topic in the world to anyone who is really seeking to be successful at anything. People are always searching for their purpose, thinking that they have some hidden purpose that they need to soul-search and find. Here is the thing: human beings are thinking things, and it's the thinking part that fucks us up. A hammer is a thing, just like a person, but a hammer does not think it simply has a simple purpose given to it by humans, and that's to hit nails. Things, by nature, perform better than we do because they do not think; they just are things that do what they are here to do, and that's it.

Not to get too philosophical, but as humans, we have the freedom to choose our purpose. Choice is purpose for an individual. We can choose what our purpose is, and once you choose, then you can move forward on performance. This is what makes being on a team so difficult—because each individual has a goal, and the team has a collective goal, and some individuals are still acting like they are looking for their purpose, avoiding their God-given ability to choose. These goals can often conflict, which most think is bad, but it is not bad; it is actually very good as long as these goals are communicated to the whole entity and all the individuals have integrity. The purpose of an individual is chosen by that individual and the purpose of an organization is chosen by the leader or leaders of that organization. If you are a coach, leader, or an owner, you are probably clear about your purpose already, but if you are not, you must get it clear now.

WHAT IS REALITY?

We as human beings are thinking things; that is to say that we are things that can think. Because we have this amazing ability, we lose touch with reality. Nobody knows what reality is; hence we can not create what we want. These short few paragraphs will get you back in touch with reality so that you, your team, or your organization can create the desired performance.

What is reality? Right now, you are thinking about all the things you consider reality to be. Most people will say things like "Perception is reality," "Reality is consciousness," "Reality is this," or "Reality is that." First, before we move on, I want you to be clear about what reality is for you. What is reality for you?

Now let's look at a scenario. Let's say you are in the middle of a street, and a bus is about to hit you. Is the bus real? Now, I always get a smart ass that will say, "Oh, well, I can choose to perceive the bus as something else." Look, it doesn't matter what you perceive the bus to be; if it hits you, you will get seriously hurt or die. Is the bus real? You bet your ass it is. But what is it about the bus that makes it real? This is the part people are missing. What makes the bus real is the fact that the bus is physical. The bus is a thing. People are also things, but they are things that think; therefore, they trick themselves into thinking that they are not things. Things that are real are physical and measurable, just like the results you want are physical and measurable. We are going to insert later that performance is whatever you say it is. And later, we will go deeper on your word and language, but for now, we are still on reality. So, reality is physical, measurable, takes up a distance and has form. With this fact, we can say that performance is created in action and action only. Nothing else dictates reality.

In Neuroscience, it has been proven that the brain neurons that create our actions are not working on their own; they are also working with and connected to neurons that dictate perception. That means our perception and actions are directly correlated with each other. Reality can only be impacted by action, but action is impacted by and directly correlated with our perception. So, the key to performance is getting a hold of our perception so we can act in a way that will impact the world and create the results we want. The way to do that is through our language. Language creates our perceptions, and our perceptions create our actions, and those actions impact reality. This may not be new to you; you know that your language is important and creates your perception, but how powerful is your language? Moving forward, we will also add that who you are is what you say you are, and the workability of a person comes down to the integrity of that person's word. Without integrity, nothing will work.

WHO ARE YOU?

So, who are you and what is an individual? This is another one of those hard questions that thinking beings such as ourselves make super difficult. But that's my gift; I can simplify things and get to the bottom of them. So, let's start with a simple question: "Who are you?" As you think about all the things you are, I am willing to bet you had thoughts such as these. "I am," then you inserted a concept. I am a cool guy or girl,

I am a hard worker, I am this, or I am that. Did all those types of thoughts come up for you? It's what we call representative language—you're using language to represent something. I also want you to notice that those thoughts come from a voice in your head.

You said all the things you are when you answered the question "Who are you?" Also, I want you to notice how nothing you said about yourself has anything to do with what you are made of. You said nothing to yourself about having a brain or bones or muscles or cells, etc. That is because we are thinking beings that think too damn much, and when we think, we think ideas, and this can keep us from workability because we think we are an idea.

The material of an individual is its body, but that is not who you are. You are "whatever you say you are," which also leads us to another major point. Here is a new definition of performance that you need to cultivate: Performance is whatever you say it is. The team is whatever the leader says it is. The organization is whatever the leaders say it is. We are a body made of material, just like a bicycle wheel is made of material, but the difference between a bicycle wheel and a person is, people are not their bodies; they are who they say they are. Individuals and organizations are created in language. Language is the house of performance. If an individual or an organization is created in language, then that would mean the integrity of a person or an organization is based on that person's or organization's word. Integrity is a matter of a person's word; nothing more, nothing less.

BROKEN

The reason why teams do not live up to their potential is that they simply are out of integrity, and what we mean by 'out of integrity' is, they are not congruent with their word. The players on your team do not do what they say, the coaches do not do what they say, and the leaders do not do what the hell they say. You know you should do what you say, but you don't because you are so broken that you can not even work properly to start doing what you say. Your shit is broken, and now that you know your shit is broken, let's fix it.

It is not as simple as doing what you say you will do. It gets a little deeper than that because it is impossible to do what you say all the time. We have made a system that keeps people upholding their integrity at all times, even when they can not do what they say. This is huge for you, your team, or your life. This is why shit does not work—everybody is walking around out of integrity. The world does not work, not because of all these ideas we have but simply because people are out of integrity.

People are divided, not whole and not complete because their word holds no power. You can instantly fix this, and once you do—as an athlete, a team, or an organization—your opportunity for performance will increase immediately, and your performance will jump to its potential as well. When this is done properly, all the things you say about performance will come to reality.

THE INTEGRITY PERFORMANCE ANOMALY

Athletes—while they are disciplined in making sure they practice, work hard, and show up—often times are sacrificing integrity in their everyday life; therefore, they are reducing their performance without being aware of it. How can this happen? If having integrity is so productive, then why don't people actually practice it? Why do people always sacrifice their integrity and live with the consequences that come from it? Why are we blind to these dramatic effects and decrease to our performance? The reason is that people are ignorant of this super important anomaly owing to the following seven causes:

CAUSE #1: Integrity is a value. To most people and on most teams, integrity is seen as a value rather than an actual necessary need for performance. People look at integrity as a judgment rather than a must. Gas is needed to run a car; that is a fact. But if gas was looked at as just some value or judgment, then the person operating the car may or may not put gas in it. If they do not put gas in, guess what? The car will not work. The same goes for performance. If integrity is not present, you will not work. Integrity is a must. Without integrity, nothing works.

CAUSE #2: Lack of self-awareness. Most people can not see when they are out of integrity because all they see is their own excuses, justifications, and rationalizations of why they could not keep their word. UnBounded Athletes do not give a fuck about explanations; we care about our word and actions, and that's it.

I was late to work one day, and my boss asked me why I was late. I told her that I had car trouble. She said, "Oh, OK. What happened to your car?" I said, "Yeah, I didn't get in it on time to get here." She laughed and asked, "Really, why are you late?" I responded, "I AM LATE BECAUSE I AM LATE." She wanted a reason so bad she could not understand why I would not give her one. Yes, it may be true that I was late because my tire was flat, but that does not impact the result. If I was late because I chose to or because there was an earthquake, the result is still the same.

UnBounded Athletes only care about the result; we do not care about—or deal in—explanations. This is so hard because we love explanations, and we also live in a blind world where everybody wants an explanation for everything. The truth only lies in reality, and reality is in the result. We will get deeper on this super important fact later, but as an UnBounded Athlete, UnBounded Coach, or UnBounded Leader, start taking 100% responsibility for your word and outcomes now!!!

CAUSE #3: Integrity is keeping one's word. Lots of people think that integrity is to just keep one's word, but there are times when it is just not possible to keep one's word. That is why we say that "integrity is a matter of one's word." When you believe integrity is to keep your word, and it becomes impossible to keep your word, or if you just flat out do not feel like keeping your word (which is fine), what happens is, you will try to conceal the fact that you are not keeping your word. Concealing the fact that you will not be keeping your word adds to the integrity performance anomaly and violates the law of integrity. Our system fixes that and keeps the integrity of your word by making sure you communicate your lack of keeping your word. By communicating this, you will keep your actual word whole, complete and undivided.

CAUSE #4: Fear of communicating that you are not keeping your word. We are all bounded by societal ideas, which makes us fearful of looking a certain way. We are all fearful of not looking good in other people's eyes. And since most people think integrity is doing what you say you will do, we often times are afraid of communicating when we are not able to do what we said we were going to do. We subconsciously feel like we lose respect when we are not able to keep our word. So, we try to avoid the threat we feel from not looking good when we do not keep our word by trying to hide it (like we did when we were a child) instead of looking at it as a challenge to fix whatever breakdown was present. Do not hide the fact you will not keep your word or did not keep your word; share it and fix it.

CAUSE #5: Integrity is not seen as a factor in performance. Most people fail to recognize that the lack of integrity actually directly impacts their performance. Society has so many false causes and dogmatic rationalizations that it's extremely hard to see that integrity is the actual answer to performance. This, in turn, conceals the law of integrity, the lack of workability, and the loss of performance that comes from being out of integrity.

CAUSE #6: Not having a desired outcome before giving one's word. When you give your word, you must be willing to actually do what you say. If your word is not tied to a desired outcome, you will not want to do it, and you will lack the power to do that thing you gave your word to. We all know we hate doing things that we do not want to do, so why do we still give our word to these things? Yes, we do have to do things we do not want to do, but if those things will move us closer to an actual desired result we want, then we will do it and learn to love it. Also, when we are after a desired result, when things get hard, we still have the motivation to do it. When you give your word to do something you do not really want to do and something difficult comes up, you will use that difficult thing as an excuse to not do it; then you will conceal why you did not do it with excuses. You can skip all that by not giving your word in the first place.

CAUSE #7: Not doing a cost-benefit analysis of exalting one's word. Most people do not know what it actually costs them when they do not exalt their word, or they do not know the benefits of actually doing it. The major keys to creating anything you want is trust, as you will see later in the book. When you dwell in the world of rationalizing and making excuses, trust is lost. Not just trust form others but also your own trust in yourself as well. Trust is essential in generating power. Trust comes from being real, from communicating, and from exalting your word.

INTEGRITY THE NEW MODEL

Integrity is a matter of your word; nothing more, nothing less. This works two ways: the first way is my word to myself, and the second way is my word to others. If I say that I am going to do something, and I do not do it, I am literally breaking myself. Not being congruent with my word is like taking spokes from a center of a bicycle wheel, fucking up my ability to work. The pronoun 'I' lives in language; therefore, my language must be impeccable to keep 'I' whole and complete. Even when it comes to "Actions speak louder than words," the focus is not on the action we live; it is what is said about the action that people live. At the end of the day, it is the context or the story that is the defining factor, and the story and context will only be believed when someone trusts your language. The trust of language is built with integrity.

THE LAW OF INTEGRITY

Integrity is a law, just like the law of gravity or any other law. It is a positive law, meaning that it is always working. Now that we have defined integrity, let's give you its law. The law of integrity states that "if integrity declines, workability declines; and when workability declines, the opportunity for performance declines." Let's give an example.

I want you to search your experience for times where this has applied to you as we go through this example. How many times have you said you were going to do something and did not do it? Small stuff like "I am going to wash the dishes," "I am going to take out the trash," or "I am going to call my mom or dad?" Let's look at things a little bit bigger, like "I am going to read every day," "I am going to eat better," or "I am going to get more reps in." And you didn't do shit. Doing this is like taking spokes out of the middle of a wheel, taking away its ability to work.

So, when you get the ball in clutch time, and you say "I am going to hit this shot" or "I am going to make this play," you have a higher chance of failing. Why? Because you do not work; your word is not complete or whole. Why would your mind trust you in clutch time when you don't even do what you say during the small times? This is the key; having integrity will dramatically raise your performance. Look at the best players to ever play; they were all congruent, and they never cheated themselves. You have a job to do, and you need to work to do that damn job. Get clear about the job and have integrity—use your word to create it.

THERE WAS THE WORD

"In the beginning was the word, and the word was with you, and the word was you." What is language? What is the word? Who knows? I would argue that our word is just expressed intent. Intent is what we say we are going to do. If you are a basketball team who intends to win a championship, but you do not even execute small intentions, how in the hell are you going to create the power to win a championship? The difference between a player like Kobe, who has such a powerful will to take over a game, and another player is integrity. Kobe has the most integrity I have ever seen in an athlete. He did what he said, and when he didn't do what he said he would do, he owned up to it. I remember, in the playoffs, Kobe had so many technical fouls that if he got one more, he would be suspended for a game. A reporter brought this up to Kobe and said, "Are you worried that you can not get any more technical fouls because your team needs you?" Kobe replied with straight power, "I will not get another one." And guess what? He didn't. Kobe can say what he is going to do, and he follows through, while most people do not have the power to do this. Why do you think Kobe got more championships after Shaq left the Lakers? It's because he 'said' he would.

THE SIX ASPECTS OF THE WORD

There are six aspects of one's word. When these aspects are whole and complete, a person or team is whole and complete.

ASPECT #1: WHAT YOU SAID: Whatever you have said you will do or will not do, and you will do it in the time you said you will do it.

ASPECT #2: WHAT YOU KNOW: Whatever you know to do or know not to do, do it as you know it's meant to be done and do it on time. Unless you have said that you are not going to do it.

ASPECT #3: WHAT IS EXPECTED: Do what is expected of you and do it on time unless you have said that you are not going to do it.

ASPECT #4 WHAT YOU SAY IS SO: Whenever you have given your word to others as to the existence of something or some state of the world, your word includes being willing to be held accountable that the others would find your evidence makes what you have asserted valid for themselves.

ASPECT #5: WHAT YOU STAND FOR: Whether said to others as a declaration or a declaration to yourself as well as what you hold yourself out to others as standing for.

ASPECT #6: THE MORAL, ETHICAL, AND LEGAL

STANDARDS OF SOCIETY: What society considers to be morally, ethically, and legally right or wrong unless you communicate that you will not live by societal standards and you accept the consequences of your choice.

EXAMPLES OF BEING OUT OF INTEGRITY

As individuals, we regularly:

- make promises and commitments we do not keep; late or non-delivery of tasks.
- show up late and/or not prepared for meetings or don't show up at all.
- surreptitiously read documents, answer emails, work on other matters while in meetings.
- fail to return telephone calls when promised.
- violate or play games with negotiated agreements.
- lie to others, including our spouses, children, partners, friends, organizations (including not being straight when it is merely uncomfortable to do so).
- cheat on spouses, cheat on taxes.
- steal (e.g., keep the excess change mistakenly given at the checkout counter or padding expense reports).
- fail to return found items even when the identity of the owner is clear.
- use the web for personal reasons while working, including shopping online, and on and on.

KEEPING YOUR WORD IS IMPOSSIBLE

It is not possible to always keep your word; that is one of the big errors of all these people who preach that you should always keep your word. Someone who always keeps their word is playing small, and we do not play small; we play big. You are a winner like me, or you would not be reading this book. You do not play small; you just needed some small distinctions so you can have more performance. Even if you do play small, it is just not flat out possible to keep your word all the time, and so, people are losing power and workability constantly because they believe they need to keep their word. Our model says that integrity is a matter of your word, not that we should always keep our word. It is not possible to always keep your word, but it is possible to always keep your word whole, complete and undivided. But how do we do this? Easy—by exalting your word.

EXALTING YOUR WORD

Integrity is a matter of your word; nothing more, nothing less. This means: do what the fuck you say. But it is not possible to do what you say all the time. I mean, let's be honest; sometimes things happen, and we should not dwell on breakdowns of our word. This is why I have developed a way to keep your word whole and complete all of the time—by exalting your word.

Exalt is defined as holding something in a very high regard.

I want you to hold your word in a higher regard than anything else, even your actions. Yes, even your actions. Actions are actions; we use our language to act as we want to, but after the act is over, it's over—it's gone. Your word will always remain. So, how do you exalt your word? How do you hold your word above all? It is very simple.

THESE ARE ALL A PROCESS OF COMMUNICATION:

STEP #1: KEEP YOUR WORD AND KEEP IT ON TIME!!!

STEP #2: JUST AS SOON AS YOU BECOME AWARE THAT YOU WILL NOT BE KEEPING YOUR WORD (INCLUDING NOT KEEPING YOUR WORD ON TIME), SAY TO EVERYONE IMPACTED, "I WILL NOT BE KEEPING MY WORD."

TELL EVERYONE IMPACTED THAT YOU WILL NOT BE KEEPING YOUR WORD AND ...

THAT YOU WILL KEEP THAT WORD IN THE FUTURE, AND BY WHEN, OR THAT YOU WILL NOT BE KEEPING THAT WORD AT ALL AND ...

WHAT YOU WILL DO TO DEAL WITH THE IMPACT ON OTHERS FOR YOUR FAILURE TO KEEP YOUR WORD OR KEEP IT ON TIME.

This is a direct access and an actionable way to keep your word whole and complete. When you apply this to your life, not just sports but all things will dramatically increase your performance. Now let's talk about the six aspects of your actual word.

This is a big fucking deal; it is everything when it comes to performance. Without integrity, nothing works, LITERALLY. So, I want to drill it into your head here.

To be a person of integrity, you must do a cost-benefit analysis before giving your word.

Since you are a person of integrity, you will think seriously and carefully before you put yourself at risk by giving your word. You must never give your word to two or more things that are not mutually consistent.

Being a person of integrity starts with giving your own word to yourself—that you will be a person of integrity. This is something you either must do or not do; there is no trying. Do it.

This is an actionable pathway to upholding your integrity so that you and your organization work. This is an actionable way to always have an opportunity for performance, depending on the performance you are creating. This is a simple system that if applied, will make your potential immediately rise to the level it should be at.

THE POTENTIAL ACCELERATOR

This is an actionable way to realize your potential immediately. You need to establish a system to apply this idea to yourself, to your team, and to your organization. A system that allows you to stay as whole and complete as possible will keep you at a level of power which will allow you to be at your best and perform at an epic level. This system will establish your completeness and increase workability, and once you're working properly, everything you say about performance will manifest quickly. There are other things that accelerate your potential, like authenticity, taking responsibility, and finding something to fight for. This is the foundation I require the athletes I coach to have so that when we dive into the ideas, those ideas actually work. I have a system I use to create UnBounded Athletes that takes athletes' performance to a crazy high level. I call this system the Tetrahedron. One of the foundations of that structure is integrity.

BEING IN THE STANDS VS BEING ON THE COURT

There are two types of languages that we use as human beings. The first type is the representative language. This is where we use language to represent something. For example, someone might say, "I want to lose weight" or "I need to work harder" or "I should practice more." These are just representations of an internal state and have no power. I call this kind of language 'being in the stands'; I call it that because it's almost like you being a reporter or a fan and saying to yourself what should be going on in the game: he should work on that shot, she should run harder, he could have done that better, etc.

Being in the stands or using language to represent has no value whatsoever. If integrity is doing what you say, then how can a statement like "I should lose weight" help anything at all? "I should lose weight" is not an action; it represents an action; therefore, it has no power. This language is a word-to-world fit, meaning we use our words to fit what we see in the world. If you listen to most people, you will observe that we all use this language as if we are in the stands and never on the court. You are an athlete, you are a coach, you are a leader; your language brings things into being. You don't say "We should"; you say "We are."

The second is the creative language, which is language that brings into being something that was not going to happen until you said it was going to happen. "I am going to make this shot"; "You are going to win this game"; "We are going to win the championship this year." Creative language does not represent anything, and it is not in the stands. Creative language actually brings things into existence and only happens on the court. This is not a word-to-world fit, but it is actually a world-to-word fit, meaning we are making the world fit our word. What we mean by 'on the court' is, it's in the domain of action.

Have you ever noticed that when you're in the zone, you are not aware of yourself? You're just so deep in the zone it's almost like you're not even there; you're just present in the game acting. This is a state of consciousness that Mihaly Csikszentmihalyi calls 'flow.' I would argue that it is not a state of consciousness at all, but that's another conversation. This is a state where you are so present in action that you are not aware of anything; you're just acting.

In order to create with your language and create something that was not going to happen before you said it was, you must gain access to the power of language beyond the mere accurate representation of the world as it already exists. Rather than just using language to represent, you have to learn to use language to bring things into existence. When you use creative language, your statements (whether accurate or not) are considered an assertion. For an assertion to be valid, the listener must believe what is asserted. Can you see now why integrity is important? You need to believe what you say to yourself, and you also want others to believe what you say as well. For example, a promise is not speaking about a promise, but you are promising. A promise is performative; it does actually perform. A promise is a specific action or a specific result at a specific time.

Creative language has three aspects for it to work:

#1: "What" - This is the action or result you will perform.

#2: "To Whom" - This is to whom you're going to do the action. Is it yourself or others?

#3: "By When" - A specific time that you will do the action or result.

COMMITMENT ALONE DOESN'T WORK

Commitments alone do not work at all. A commitment is not going to realize a created future. Once the created future is articulated, what it takes to realize that future is action and action alone. The source of performance is action; nothing more, nothing less.

For action to take place, you will need an opportunity to take action and a method for managing with integrity the execution of the required action.

Talk is cheap only for those whose word exists in a place that does not give them a reliable opportunity for the keeping of their word and on time.

A QUESTION TO PONDER

So, I have a transformational question for you to ponder: Where does your word go after you have closed your mouth? As an athlete, coach, leader, owner, where does your word go when you are done talking? Answer that question, create some goals, say what you are going to do with integrity, and I guarantee you will realize your potential.

LEARN THE MOST VALUABLE SKILLS AND DISTINCTIONS THAT WILL GET YOUR TEAM, ORGANIZATION, OR ATHLETES TO PERFORM AT THEIR PEAK POTENTIAL AND INCREASE THEIR POTENTIAL MORE THAN ANYTHING

Performing at your best is the most valuable skill you can learn as an athlete, coach, or leader, and the Tetrahedron performance system is the system to help you learn those skills and distinctions in record time.

The Tetrahedron is a step-by-step system based on the combined experience of the best mindset coaches. Roy has been studying mindset for a decade and has been helping athletes, teams, and organizations perform on higher levels.

The Tetrahedron includes tools to help you and your team overcome mental blocks, get an opportunity to perform at world-class greatness-type levels and increase in game production.

This program includes worksheets and templates that will coach you and your organization to keep performance at high levels and leave room for higher levels of performance to show up. Implementing this system and tools will take your organization from good to great in a short amount of time.

Learn more by emailing Roy at roy@RoyRedd.com. Roy will come and talk to your team or organization to train you on how to reach your peak potential in an instant with his Potential Accelerator.

www.ingramcontent.com/pod-product-compliance
Lightning Source LLC
Chambersburg PA
CBHW061547250726
48657CB00006B/2341